life isn't made for

Perfect People:

Book 2

Topher Kearby

Cover Art by Topher Kearby
Art Copyright © 2022 by Topher Kearby
Cover Design Copyright © 2022 by Topher Kearby
www.TopherKearby.com

Cover Design by Jeremiah Lambert
www.JeremiahLambertArt.com

Edited by Christina Hart
Additional Editing by Whitney Weber
Formatted & Proofread by Christina Hart

ISBN: 978-0-578-38146-6

First Edition
Printed in the United States of America
by Gray Force Publishing

Letter to the Reader:

There are some that are born into the light. And then there are some, like me, who have to fight their way out of the darkness. It's a coin flip. It's a lottery. It's life experiences and everything in between. But the truth is we're all built differently. With different parts and pieces. Different mental makeups and physical traits.

I remember the first time I had a conversation with someone who didn't struggle with anxiety or depression. I didn't know that some people were different than me. I thought everyone had the same issues and fought the same battles. And at that moment I realized it wasn't true. And to be honest, I was jealous.

Because carrying the weight of a mind that plays tricks on you is heavy. It's as if you're constantly on guard from an attack. But not from an outside force; from yourself. Being so alert and so aware can drain you. And not everyone feels that way.

And that's why not everyone understands the reality of a brain on fire.

I've put in a lot of work. On myself. To be where I am today.

But I still have a long way to go.

I get angry because the person I've worked so hard to leave behind still shows up from time to time. And I recognize his face. And I hear the way he speaks. And I'm ashamed. And that's the truth.

It's not an easy journey, this thing called life. It challenges you and pushes you to recognize that you *can* be better.

I've caught myself saying, "That's just the way I am." As if that's a blanket excuse for me to be worse than I could be. I'm notoriously hard on myself. I realize that. But for the first time in a very long time, there is clarity in my vision. I see who I want to be and I'm becoming that person step by step.

It's challenging. It's uncomfortable.

But it's also worth it.

If my work could speak one truth to people, it would be that you are loved, you are appreciated, you are seen, and you are not alone.

-Topher

Life Isn't Made For Perfect People

Life isn't made for perfect people.
It's made for those
who know how to turn an impossible
situation into something beautiful.
It's made for fighters, dreamers,
lovers, and people who won't give up
even when life feels impossible.

It's not perfect.
It's not easy.

But that's why we're made
so damn tough.

Part 1:

The New

Writing

I've said it before and here
I am again saying the same thing:
writing a book like this is difficult.
It takes a lot out of me each time.
Even this small little thing.
Because I don't know how to write
anything but my heart, from my gut.

It is all fire and glass.
It is all revelation and resentment.
It is all life reexamined.

And I'm far more comfortable forgetting.

Hello,
Anxiety.

I acknowledge
you, I feel you
inside my chest,
but it is time
for you to move
on. I claim this
day. I own these
moments. My hope
is greater than
my fears.

Pages Of Therapy

The older I get the more my words
get sealed up inside my guts.
I just don't talk that much.
Maybe at a certain point in life we all
just get tired of hearing ourselves speak.
We just choose to say less.

I choose to say less.

So, here I am again writing.
Hoping this process breaks
loose my true feelings from
the cage that life's routine
has placed them in.

Swim

Hiding from the pain works for a while.
If we keep busy enough,
If we don't stop long enough to breathe.
But then we do stop.
And it all comes crashing back against us
like the waves of the sea.
And we drown.

Better to learn to swim with the waves.

We're All Happier

"You seem happier. What's changed?"

At a certain point I realized I was using all my time trying to be someone who made everyone else happy. But I made myself miserable doing that.

"And now?"

Now I am myself. The people who love me appreciate that I'm opening up more. And I'm thankful they understand. We're all happier.

Friends With Peace

I am nothing if I am not broken. I am
fake if I am found. My real self rests
in the fires. I am only alive when I am on
my way out.

This is me. Those words up there clicking
across the screen like marching ants. I
can feel the letters in my blood like acid
dripping from an IV. That's the pain of an
artist and also the beauty.

I was married to these ideas. I was ready to
die with these beliefs.
But no more.

My pain is not my only fuel for creation.
My brokenness is not the only color that
paints the sky.

I am now sitting down with peace and
asking her to help me learn.
It's a long process. It might take the rest
of my life to fully understand.
But I am willing.

Because too many have been burned up
letting the fires of brokenness fuel their
creativity. I don't judge. Yet,
I don't desire to be ash.

I will be friends with peace.

I'll keep
breathing
and you'll keep
breathing
and together
we'll stay alive.

Listen

Green and yellow lights
swim over my skin like an ocean.
I am floating,
I am above the trees now,
I am one with whatever
or whoever
is more than me.

The universe is calling.

And I am finally
willing to listen.

Start Something New

Today is the right day
to start something new.
To plan that trip you've
always wanted to take.
To make that change you
know you need to make.

Today is the day.
And it's a good day.

Next

I look ahead toward the future
and for the first time I can't
see what's next.

That's a scary feeling.

Who am I without a future
that I'm working toward?

I'm not sure I know.

But I plan to find out.

Gift

Life is a gift. We know this. Yet, it's hard
to stop and understand what that really
means. It often doesn't feel like a gift.
Some days are unwanted and just plain
miserable. Who would want a cold, wet
Monday? Probably someone who doesn't have
any Mondays left.

"Thanks, Dad."
You're welcome.

Yes, that's a simple answer. Who wants a
bad version of something good? Always
someone who doesn't have anything left.
But, there is a powerful truth in that way
of thinking. It's the same idea that's been
around since the beginning of time. We
look at what we have and we want it to be
better because we think we deserve it to be
better, but that isn't how life works.

We don't earn better days just because
we've been better.

Fall in love
with the one
who helps
you carry the
world when
everything
becomes too
heavy.

Known

I think there are just a couple
of people in life who really get you.

Maybe a lover or a friend.
Your mom or your brother.
Somebody on the internet.
I think about that a lot
and it gives me peace.

I don't need to be known by everyone.
I don't want to be known be everyone.

Because I know I am known.
And that's good.

Stubborn

I'm stubborn to a fault.

But if I love you
then I love you.

And if you need me
then I'll be there.

I can't promise more
than that.

The problem
with being a
slow processor
is that by the
time you've
worked through
everything,
everyone else
has already
moved on.

Expectations

I want to be isolated.
I want to heal on my own.
But my heart bleeds out.
All over everything and everyone.
Until it's impossible to hide.
So I speak before I'm ready.
Words that haven't been given
time to ripen.
They are sharp and bitter.

And you say, "You're cold.
Your words are ice."

And I say, "I'm sorry."

But what I want to say is,
"What did you expect?"

Cowboy

I feel like I should have
been a cowboy, though I don't
really know how to ride a horse
or mend a fence.

I've ridden a horse, of course.
It's the mending where I struggle
most. I typically just tear it down
and build it all over again.

No wonder I'm so tired.

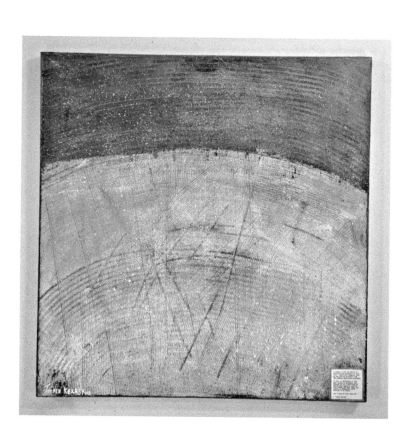

Muddy boots by
the back door
and fresh
flowers on the
front porch,
that sounds like
a good life
to me.

Love & Lies

Spit gravel,
my friends.
And tell no lies.

Unless those lies
are about love.

Because who understands
how that works anyway.

I love the
difficult
parts of people.

The ones we're
too afraid
to reveal to
anyone else.

Routine.
That word and I
aren't friends.

This page is for you. Write your poem here.
Whatever you want to write. If you post it
on social media, tag me in it and I'll do my
best to share it.

Part 2:

Country Songs

Not Afraid

I'm not afraid to die,
but I am afraid to cry,
because crying reminds me
I'm alive.

The tears in the eyes,
the cheeks wet with water,
the days spent missing the mark
and nights getting darker.

I'm not afraid to die
but I'm afraid to cry
because crying reminds me
I'm alive.

I've seen death the least,
and I've seen tears the most,
but every time I feel them on my face
it's like I've seen my own ghost.

I'm not afraid to die,
but I am afraid to cry,
because crying reminds me
I'm alive.

Gravel

I trust people with gravel
in their voices,
like they swallowed some pain
along the way.

Those people carry regret in their eyes
and honesty in their words,
but never seem to say too much
to anyone they might hurt.

Life rips and it shreds,
and sometimes we can't do more
than just take a bite and swallow.
It changes us, becomes part of us,
and fills up what once was hollow.

I trust people with gravel
in their voices,
like they swallowed some pain
along the way.

Because at least
those people are honest,
and not some sucker
playing the same old game.

I Think

I think I'm going to jail someday
after I've had too much to drink.
I think I'll end up in prison someday
when I've had too much time to think.

I'll plan,
I'll stew,
I'll fight,
and I'll swear,
all because the world I imagined
was never really there.

Because this world isn't fair
and it never really was,
just giving you enough hope
for a late-night kind of buzz.

You won't hear me complaining
about the cell or the cinderblock walls,
because at least I'll be in the place
where I felt I already was.

I think I'm going to jail someday
after I've had too much to drink.
I think I'll end up in prison someday
when I've had too much time to think.

The Way Things Was

Maybe we just need
an old truck
and a new us
to get things back to the way we was.

I know what you're thinking—
that ain't no way to speak,
it's were not was,
and then you'd smile
and take a sip from your drink.

Wild free spirits
and a wide-open life to dream,
two hearts,
one purpose,
our unstoppable misfit team.

So let's buy that old truck
we always said we would
and get things back to
the way we know we could.

Maybe we just need
an old truck
and a new us
to get things back to the way we was.

This page is for you. Write your poem here.
Whatever you want to write. If you post it
on social media, tag me in it and I'll do my
best to share it.

Part 3:

The Hits

Imperfectly

In a perfect world
perhaps there would
be a perfect time
to fall in love,
but that world does
not exist.

So, let us
love the best we can—
imperfectly.

Fall in love and
make mistakes.
Life is too short
for perfection.

Missing It

Are you awake?

"Can't sleep."

What's on your mind?

"My past mistakes. My future dreams."

What about your present?

"I'm worried that I'm missing it."

Forgive Yourself

"I should have said it differently.
I was too rushed, too harsh, and
I wasn't thinking."

You have to forgive yourself.

"I can't. Not yet. I need to make
it right. I HAVE TO FIX IT."

*You already apologized. You
did the right thing. We are all
just human. We are made to
make mistakes.*

"I couldn't do this life without
you. You know that, right?"

I know. I love you. Now come to bed.

Let's set aside
our insecurities
today and just
love each other.

Paycheck To Paycheck

Mental illness is a lot like living
paycheck to paycheck.

Most days you're okay.
The end of the month may be a bit
sketchy. And then when emergency
strikes everything could fall apart
really quickly.

Beautiful Fight

"I'm worried."

About?

"Everything. What if what
I'm doing doesn't matter?
Maybe I'm wasting my time.
I just feel like giving up."

*It may not get any easier.
In fact, it may get harder
every day until the end of
our days. But that's the
beautiful part of life—
the fight.*

My pain has
brought me here,
so I will listen
to what it wants
to teach me.

Geared Low

I am not down nor am I depressed;
I am geared low.

I work through ideas slowly,
I think about life deeply,
and I am in no hurry to speed
through the difficult times;
that's when I grow.

Beautiful Dangers

What beautiful
dangers hide
within my mind.
What brilliant
secrets line the
delicate structure
of my soul.

All of these
wonderfully
terrible pieces
of me—the
shadowed portions
that make me whole.

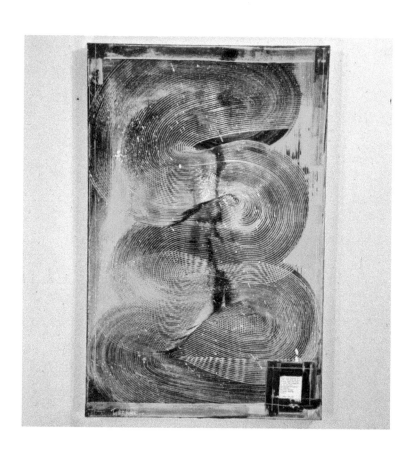

It's easier to
drown our minds
in noise than it
is to have honest
conversations
with ourselves
in silence.

All Out Of Words

You look like you have a lot
on your mind.

"It's been a long day."

Want to talk about it?

"No. I'm all out of words.
I just want to sit with you
for a while and watch the stars
light up the sky."

Worry

What's on your mind?

"Thinking."

Always. What about?

"Just how I've never felt comfortable being myself with anyone before. That is, until I met you."

But your face tells me you're worried.

"I am. Being this vulnerable with another person scares me."

Why?

"I guess I'm just worried it can't last."

Stuck

So often
I know what I want to say
but I can't say it, because
the words are stuck
or lost inside this maze of
a mind that I have.

It's frustrating.

Keep Going

Tell me about your day.

"I wasn't my best today.
Life took more than it
gave and I failed more
than I won."

So what's your plan?

"Get up, try again, and
keep going like that
every day until I run
out of days."

Mornings are
meant for hot
coffee & long
conversations
about dreams.

Still Healing

Maybe it hasn't been
as long as you think,
or as long as they tell
you to think.

It still hurts.
It's all still right
there.

You're still healing.
So don't rush the process
and don't listen to people
when they say to just move
on already.

You are moving on.
That stuff just
takes time.

Love The One

Fall in love with the one
who isn't willing to let
you settle in life, the
one that tells you to keep
fighting even when life is
at its worst.

To The Ends Of The Earth

To the ends of the earth.
Through the waves of the sea.
To the tallest of mountains.
I'll be with you and you'll be with me.
We'll wander together.
We'll explore and we'll roam.
If we get lost for a while
it won't matter.

Because when we're together
we'll always be home.

Truly Loving

Real love does not
love *in spite of.*
Real love loves
because of.
Because of your flaws.
Your mistakes. Your past.
And your weirdness.

If someone is *putting up
with you* then I don't think
they are truly loving you.

We often give
away oceans of
ourselves for a
single raindrop
of acceptance.

Perhaps

I think we fear love
because we fear losing
ourselves within another
person. Perhaps we will
never be the same.

Perhaps that's the point.

Reincarnation

Yes, I believe
in reincarnation.

Because I still
see you in everyone
I meet.

Wild things,
you and I,
running
breathlessly
under an
endless sky.

Hope: Part 2

Hope is the spark
that sets my heart
on fire, and it's the
fuel that keeps me
fighting for my dreams
when the rest of the
world is trying to
convince me to give up.

Find Out

"Nothing lasts forever."

Maybe not. But with
you, I plan on finding out.

We miss so
many beautiful
moments waiting
for the next.

Confetti & Congratulations

Victory does not always feel
like you expected it to feel.

Sometimes it's confetti and
congratulations.

But more often it feels like
you're trying to steady yourself
as the world starts spinning
even faster than before.

Still A Dream

The beautiful thing about
the future is that it's
still a dream. It could
be anything and everything.

That's the most
beautiful feeling.

Find The Way

It's going to be scary.
When you take that first step.
When you leave behind your past
and look ahead to your new future.
You know you're in the right place,
but that doesn't make those first
steps any easier. Or the ones
that follow those. The journey
will be filled with worry, fear,
beauty and purpose. Every emotion
we are meant to feel.

That is the design. We are meant
to wander and wonder. To step into the
unknown and say,

"I may not have it all figured out
today, but I know in my heart
that I will find a way."

It's Worth It

Pain doesn't heal overnight.
It takes time. You're making progress.
You're growing. You're making your life
better. That's amazing. You're amazing.
But still, you'll have moments
when everything will hurt.
You'll have days when the
struggle feels impossible.
You'll have thoughts that
say, *"Give up. It's over."*

But hear me out.
I understand. It's a journey,
and it's brutal and beautiful
and everything in between.

But most importantly,
it's worth it.

Starts With Love

*"How can I approach this
with love?"*

That's the question I'm asking
myself more lately. I want to
act with kindness. I want to
build a home of peace. I want
to live a life full of purpose.

And I believe that journey
starts with love.

Made To Burn

It's easy to fear your voice.
People will tell you, *"Don't say
that. Not here. Bite your
tongue. Keep your mouth shut.
People will think..."*
And so it goes.
On and on until we forget how
to speak. We nod our heads
when we want to scream.
We give up. We give in.
Because it feels easier.

But it's not easier.

Quieting your fire will just
leave you cold.

And you were made to burn.

It's difficult
to stand still
while life
catches up to the
place your heart
has already
taken you.

Stronger Stuff

When the waves come, I will
be stronger. When the darkness
falls, I will shine brighter.
When the days become heavy,
when the nights feel long,
when the starlight dims, and
the music goes quiet, I will
make it through.

Because I am made from stronger
stuff. And that stronger stuff
does not break easily.

Cereal & Tattoos

*What do you want to
do tonight?*

"Let's just eat cereal
at home and then go get
new tattoos."

Small Talk

Authentic conversations
are often painful and
can take a lot of time
to process.

But I'll take those over
pointless small talk about
nothing any day.

Imperfect Creatures

We are imperfect creatures.
We carry a lifetime of baggage
on our backs like a trader
at the market. We have relationship
scars and family issues. Insecurities
and egos that require attention. We
want to be kind but some days
we are terrible. This is the rhythm
of being human.

Then we fall in love.

We bring all of our hang-ups and lay
them at the feet of another human who
carries just as many broken bits of life
as we do. We say, "Just love me and that
will be enough."

Yet, it's more than that. It's learning
the rhythm of another body. It's
protecting another heart that is not your
own. It's feeling passionate and hurt and
lonely and hopeful.

All within the span of a moment in the sun.

It's love.

The most complicated drug.

There was
something in
the way you saw
me that made me
see the world
brand new.

Stronger

I don't have it all figured out.
Most days my life looks more mess than
masterpiece. I work two full-time jobs
to build a life for the ones I love.
Most night I still don't feel like I've done
enough, and a host of other issues from
time to time. That's real life.

That's my life.

But I'm okay. Life still feels beautiful to
me. That's the benefit of knowing your
truth and having authentic conversations
with yourself.

Life isn't getting any easier.

But I sure as hell am getting stronger.

Weird Happiness

Happiness is
being weird enough
that most people
leave you alone,
and the ones who stay
truly love you.

These People I Love

Yes, these people I love
are all a bit weird,
a bit strange, a bit loud,
and a bit off, but I
wouldn't change a thing.

We Felt Everything

The lucky ones are those
who feel too much, too often,
for seemingly no good reason.
They are how we all once began—
birthed, screaming into a world
that was so bright we could not
even open our eyes to see.

We felt everything, and needed
everything just to survive.

And it was a beautiful pain.
Now most are slaves to endless
checklists and tasks completed
over and over again.
Until to feel anything
feels as if there is something
wrong with us.

No. I say, "Hell no."
We are not broken.

We are finally fixed.

Fall in love
with the way you
make each other
laugh. Love is a
lot easier when
you know how to
take a joke.

Dust Yourself Off

Dust yourself off.
Set new plans.
Fill your heart with hope
and passion for a future
that you will make happen.
Pursue the impossible.
Make your dreams a reality.
Tough days are normal.
Falling down is normal.

So is learning to stand
back up.

All Parts Of The Day

Sunset chaser.
Late night star gazer.
Early morning coffee
drinker. And afternoon
deep thought thinker.

Finding the beauty during
all parts of the day.

Embrace Your Happiness

I am for happiness. I am
for joy. I am for people
pursuing their passions
and finding their purpose.
Whatever that might look
like. Whatever that might be.
If you're doing something
that makes life better for
you or for the people you love,
then go for it. With your
whole heart. Don't listen
to negative voices because
they just want to keep you low.
But you were born with wings
and meant to soar.

Happiness can be difficult
to find. So if you've found yours,
embrace it.

Embrace The Unknown

Be someone who isn't
afraid to take risks.
Who sees life as an
adventure. Who wakes
up on a new day and
says, "I may not know
what life has planned
for me, but I know
I'll be ready."

Embrace the unknown.
Follow your heart.
And learn just how
strong you are along
the way.

Speak to me
through music.
Let me see your
soul through the
songs that you
love. And let me
feel your heart
through the
melodies that
move you.

Music Finds You

I believe in music that finds you
when you need it most. That perfect
song that comes into your life and
moves you in a new direction or
holds you still for a while. That's a
special kind of connection that
can only be felt through music.

UFO — Take Me With You

I've always been the kind of person that
questions everything. I look up toward the
sky and see the infinite stars and I think,
"Why not?" Why shouldn't there be other
places beyond this place where life exists?
That just makes sense to me. And maybe that
life is completely different than our own
and maybe that's why we'll never interact
or never cross paths. That doesn't mean
there aren't infinite other versions of
life scattered throughout the universe.
It's fun to think about. I like to let my
imagination run wild.

When I lie down and look up at the stars, I
wonder. That's what we humans are supposed
to do—wonder, dream, hope, and speculate
about things beyond ourselves. Maybe
that's what makes us human. The ability to
dream these ridiculously impossible
dreams about the infinite. And desire some
kind of connection with the unknown.

It's a beautiful journey, this life. It's a
beautiful gift, these minutes, even though
some days can be difficult. But I'm
thankful for the curiosity that was born
in me and never left.

So, if any aliens are reading this...take me
with you.

Never Change

The world may not
"get" you. People
might call you
weird or *strange*.
That's okay.
The best people are
always seen that way.
You're a dreamer and
you see the world for
what it could be,
not for what it is.
Never change.

Your Weird

The crowd will say,
"Just be yourself."
And then you will try
and they will say,
"No, not like that."

Instead, listen to your
heart. It wants you to
be the person you are
meant to be.

Embrace your weird.

Each Other

I still believe that
love and compassion
are the best weapons
against fear and
uncertainty.

If you can help,
then help.

It's simple;
we all need each other.

Some nights I
have to remind
myself that
I am not as
broken as I
once was and
that happiness
is possible
for me.

I will live
with purpose.
I will live
with passion.
I will make
the most of
my days.

True Purpose

It will not be perfect
when you get *there*.
You will not be happier
when you own *that*.
Everything will not be
easier when you finish *it*.

True purpose starts within.

Step Forward

It doesn't need
to make sense
to everyone if
it makes sense
to you.

It's your life
and your choice.
Everything else
is just noise.

Step forward with
faith in yourself.
And you'll be
happier for it.

Stronger Through Failure

Failures do not define us.
They shape us, mold us,
and build us into stronger
versions of ourselves.

Being Human

Never be ashamed to say,
"I'm worn out. I've had enough.
I need some time for myself."

That isn't being selfish.
That isn't being weak.

That is being human.

Choose Beauty

Life is like art.

If you focus on the flaws,
that's all you will see.
If you focus on the beauty,
that's all you will see.

I choose beauty.

No Better Feeling

There is no better feeling
than when life gives you
all it has, tests you at
every corner, fights you
with every choice, and still
you stand at the end of it all.
A little worn down. A little
bloody. A little unsure of what
is coming next.

But a hell of a lot stronger
than you ever would have
imagined.

The Other Side Of Pain

Sometimes we are on the mountaintop
and sometimes we are in the valley.
That can feel defeating or quite
lonely because we think we've failed.

But we haven't.
That mountain is now behind us
and the future is ahead.
We fought and we climbed
and we made it to the other side.
The valley is our chance to recharge
and reflect before we begin our
new climb.

There is purpose on the other
side of pain. Keep going.

*Where do you
want to go?*

"Anywhere.
Everywhere.
I don't care.
Let's just go."

I'm good at
beginning
and ending.
It's the middle
where I
struggle.

Love the one
who is willing
to get dirty,
digging up the
deepest parts of
your soul.

Take Time To Remember

Sometimes I get stuck on
what I am not yet, and it
stops me in my tracks.

I want to be...
I hope this will happen...
I'm not who I thought I'd...

Then I take a minute and
rub my fingers against the
sides of my head. I breathe
long greedy breaths. And I
remember just how far I've
already come to be where I
am today.

The Good Moments

Some people aren't happy
and that's why they don't
want you to be happy.

Ignore them. If you're pumped
for something, then be pumped
for it. I woke up today excited
because I had new coffee to try.

Life is little moments,
all pushed together into years.

Don't miss them.

Don't Give Up

People who have already given up will tell
you to give up because they regret giving
up. People who are still out there fighting
for their dreams, living the life they
choose, will tell you to do the same because
they know how good it feels. When people
ask me for advice, which is their first
mistake, I tell them to go and do it.

"Where do I begin?"

Hell if I know. I'm still figuring it out.
But I know that the time I'm spending
figuring it out has been the best time of
my life.

Messy Beautiful Life

"I just feel like I mess up too much.
I say the wrong things.
I do something stupid.
It's a cycle and I'm worn out."

I get it. I feel the same way.

"Yeah?"

*Yeah. We're human. Sometimes we just screw
up, but that doesn't mean we stop living.
Being alive is an art, and it's messy.*

"Too messy."

*Maybe,
but that just makes it more beautiful.*

Invisible Distance

There is an invisible distance that you
have crossed to be in the place you are in
right now. You may not remember the
struggles, the hard work, the sacrifices,
or the pain it has taken to arrive here,
but trust me. You have overcome more than
you realize. So maybe today was a bad day
and you've forgotten your amazing
journey. If so, let me encourage you to
reflect and celebrate just how far you've
actually come.

It's breathtaking.

New Passions

Let's pursue new passions,
seek out adventures,
plan our futures as if our
lives depend on them,
and find out what we are
really made of.

Life is too short to
give our days over to fear.

Turn down
the worry
and turn up
the hope.

Syrup

I speak with rawness in my
voice at times because I
can no longer swallow the
syrupy sweet lies of this world.

Human Thing

Some days I feel like I'm
faking this *human* thing.

I look around and try to
act like other people are
acting, hoping they don't notice
how clueless and strange
I really am.

Everything & Nothing

I have this thing I do where
in the middle of doing one thing
I decide I NEED to do EVERYTHING
and then I forget about that one
thing I started out doing.

Proud Failure

Some days we fail
even though we gave
everything; that's normal.

I am a proud failure,
because at least I know
I tried. So what if it
didn't turn out? Maybe
it will next time.

No.
We do not break.
But sometimes
we bend so far
that coming
back up
takes a while.

Advice To My Younger Self: Part 1

You're going to experience some pain.
Your brain doesn't work like most people's.
You're going to fight a lot of private
battles. Challenges will come and you will
not be ready for them all.
It will hurt. You will fail.
And you'll want to give up.

But I'll also tell you this.

You're stronger than you realize.
The same mind that causes so many
struggles will also bring you a lot of joy.
You won't be alone. There will be people
who love you and they will help you
understand yourself better. Listen to
those people and tune out the negative
voices. You'll end up all right.

Life is beautiful.
Never give up.

It All Matters

Who you are is important.
Your identity. The path
you have walked. The pain
you have made it through.
The healing you are still
processing. The growth.

It all matters.

And so do you.

There is no
better feeling
than laughing
with people
you love.

Be Brave

I don't want to regret
not becoming the person
I know I could be. Just
because I'm scared to
take the risks
I know I need to take.

Life is too short to
not be brave.

Wake

Wake and dream.
Plan and hope.
Fill your mind
with wonder.
Fill your heart
with passion.

Make today the
best day of
your life.

Who You Really Are

When you have an amazing day.
When you overcome. And you
make something happen that
no one thought you could.

Write it down.
Hold on to it.

Because there will be a day
when things get hard.
Difficult. Almost impossible.
And on that day take those
words out and read them aloud.
Over and over again. And take
time to remember who you
really are.

Even through
pain, beauty
still grows.

Everyone Deserves Happiness

You don't need to make
things harder on yourself
just because you feel like you
don't deserve happiness.

Everyone makes mistakes.
Everyone has regrets.
Everyone feels like they
aren't enough sometimes.

That's normal.
That's human.

But everyone also deserves
forgiveness and understanding.

Everyone deserves to be happy.

Best Of Me

When you're working toward something.
When you're planning. When you're
dreaming. When you're putting things in
place to change your life. You will have
difficult days. And impossible moments.
And weight will sit on your chest and make
it feel as though you can't breathe. It's in
that moment that you have to decide. You
have to prove what you are really made of.
And the thing is...you already know. You
know the battles you've won. You know the
wounds you've healed. And you know the
person you are today is so much stronger
than the person you were.

So say to the impossible day,
"I see you. I feel you. I understand
why you are here. But you're not
getting the best of me. Because the
best of me is set aside for my future."

I Change In Waves

I don't change little by
little; I change in waves.

Like the ocean winds
building and growing until
they crash against the shore.
And then suddenly I am
different. I listen, and
the sounds are different.
Everything is changed in
a moment. That's what it
feels like, but I know it's
not true.

I had been growing all
along. I just finally had
the strength to break through.

There Are Those

There are those who promise
they will be there for you,
but then they never are.

And there are those who
don't need to say anything,
because they're already
standing next to you.

Stay Authentic

People will put you down
because they see something
in you that they wish they were.

Something strong.
Something beautiful.
Something authentic.

The Cycle Of Growth

When you trust someone with the deepest
most protected parts of yourself, it feels
amazing. Perhaps even freeing at first.
But there will come a day, or probably a
night, when you freak the heck out because
that level of vulnerability becomes
terrifying, and the pressure starts to
mess with your mind.

"What if?"
"What now?"
"I never should have trusted..."

Fearfully the mind rushes to judgment
like a rabbit from a wolf. It's okay. That's
the cycle of growth. But if the person you
opened up to truly loves you, then those
nights of mental questions are so worth it.

It's a gift to feel comfortable with
another human. Don't throw it away
because of fear.

Beautiful And Pure

Life is so beautiful and pure at times.

It's as if fresh air fills your lungs
and you can truly breathe. During
those moments you are reminded of all
the wonders that surround you and how
grateful you are to experience each one.

Treasure those times.

Hold them close.

For those moments of magic
give life its meaning.

Never Give Up

I've been down.
And I've been out.
I've met challenges
that overwhelmed me.
I've had moments that
became too heavy to
carry on my own.
I've fallen.
I've quit.
I've made a fool
of myself.
I've been counted out.

But I'm still here.
Standing. Fighting.
Dreaming. And making
the most of my days.

That's something to
be proud of.

Never give up.

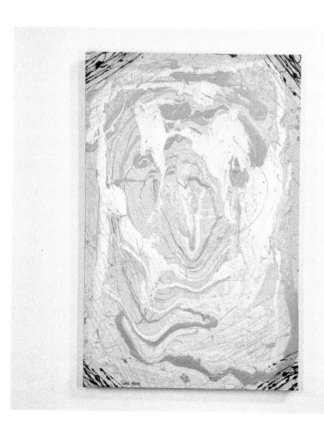

When I am
surrounded by
the beauty and
power of nature,
I feel more in
tune with my
true self.

Painful Ache

It's a painful ache
to want more
than you are wanted,
to need more
than you are needed,
and to be forgotten
when all you can do
is remember.

Nothing clears
my mind more
than a long
drive on a warm
summer night.

Favorite T-Shirt

Sometimes just putting
on your favorite t-shirt
makes you feel like anything
is possible.

The Perfect Plan

Let's put our phones
down,
turn the music
up,
and get lost just enough
to find ourselves again.

I feel calm
amidst the
chaos; I feel
lost when I am
standing still.

Hold Me

Hold me now
for just a little
while longer.

Let's let the
starlight
wash away
our worries
for the night.

Valuable

You deserve to be with
someone who values your
time and understands how
lucky they are to have you
as part of their life.

Protect Your Joy

If it makes you happy
then I'm for it.

Like watching Christmas
movies in July?
Go hiking in the rain?
Buy Lucky Charms just to eat the
marshmallow bits?
Or anything else that doesn't hurt
anyone else?

Then go for it.

Don't let other people steal your joy.

Trust

"How can you tell someone
that you truly love them?"

I trust you with all of me.

To Be Heard

I think there are a lot of people
who just ache to be heard. To be
truly listened to. To be understood.

That's the power of real conversations.

They can change someone's life.

Rare Comfort

Always such a comfort when
someone sees the real you.
And loves that person first.
There is never a need to
hide your stripes or filter
your thoughts around such a love.
It's pure. It's beautiful.
It's rare.

If you know such a comfort
then consider yourself a
lucky one.

There are times
when pain rolls
down our cheeks,
and there are
times when it is
love. Those tears
make us human.

The Misfits

I prefer the misfits.
The weird ones. The
broken and the strange.

It's the rest of the
world that I struggle
to understand.

Let's just
get the hell
out of here
for a while
and see
somewhere
new.

Quit giving
away the best of
who you are for
people who give
you their
leftovers.

Preparing To Be Strong

Feeling broken isn't romantic.
It's painful and full of empty
days and too-long nights.
No one wants to be shattered.
Pieces tossed to the wind like
unwanted scraps of sand. We all
want to feel whole—complete.
And that just takes time.
Breathe. Renew your spirit.

The broken are not weak;
they are just preparing
to be strong.

Comfortable Alone

I think some of us
are most comfortable alone
because we are hypersensitive
of other people's needs.

"Is this music too loud?"
"Is this food okay?"
"Are you having fun?"
"Are you happy?"

And on and on
until we exhaust ourselves
by just being ourselves;
we just care so much.

Working On It

I have this bad habit of sabotaging good
things in my life. I'll find something
negative about whatever it is and
then focus on that until it all falls
apart. And then I'm like, *"Yep, I knew it
wouldn't work out."*

It's some kind of strange protective act
that I do in order to keep myself from
being heartbroken or disappointed again.
Things don't always work out, but that
doesn't mean they never will or haven't
before. I need to remind myself that
happiness isn't a weakness and that I'm
"allowed" to feel it. Sometimes I just don't
trust "real" happiness. Like I haven't
earned it. Or I don't deserve it. I know
that's unhealthy and untrue. I need to
grow.

I'm tired of losing good things in life just
because I've been trained to see the worst
case scenario.

I want to be better.
I want to be happy.

I'm working on it.

The Power Of Hope

Yes.
Not everything went
as planned. In fact,
it all fell apart.

Terribly.
Spectacularly.

No problem.
The pieces are all still there.
I can put them back together
in a new way.

That's the power of hope.

Ever changing.
Forever growing.
Each day I am
made new.

A New Day

A new day does not
begin with the sunrise.

It begins with a new way
of thinking—fresh eyes.

To Be Here With You

I may not know you.
Not really.
But I know this world
needs you.
And I believe you're doing
a damn good job fighting
through a bit of
a tough time.

I respect your grit.
I understand your tears.
And I'm thankful to
be in a world where
you are too.

If You Can, Then Do

If you can be kind,
then be kind.
If you can show love,
then show love.
If you can help,
then help.

That's how we make
the world better.

I Believe In You

I've come to the point in my life
where I just understand people better.
At least I try. When I see anger, I also
see pain and frustration. When I see
tears, I also see growth and a willingness
to keep fighting. When I see love, I also
see all the choices that kept that love
alive. When I see...I see someone who
might just change the world.

Find someone
who loves you
for your Jekyll
and your Hyde.

Lightning

Some spend their
lives avoiding the
storms; others step
right into
the lightning.

The Old Barn

There's something about an old barn smell
that's just like all other old barns
there's ever been. And for me it reminds me
of my childhood. My time with my
grandfather. He had a couple of old barns
and they were filled with old things.
Coffee cans full of screws. Boxes
overflowing with tools. Metal and oil.
Tractors and blades that cut. It was magic.

It would be a thousand degrees in the
middle of the summer and he'd be in that
old barn working. As if the heat didn't
bother him. As if the sweat didn't soak his
red plaid shirt. That was my hero. My
grandfather. And now here I am with an old
barn of my own. And it smells the same.

There are no cans filled with screws.
There's no tractor or blades that cut. But
there will be. My daughters will grow up
knowing that old barn smell and making
their own memories on hot summer days.

And that is good. And that is life. And that
is happiness to me.

Open doors are
for quitters.
I brought a
sledgehammer.

Just Be With Me

Take a walk
with me.
Have a talk
with me.
Grab a drink
with me.
Sit and think
with me.
Be alone with
me.
Get lost with
me.

Just be,
with me.

Some People

Some people make
everything better.
Heavy days seem
lighter. Dark nights
feel brighter. And
it's easier to carry
the weight of it all
when they are around.

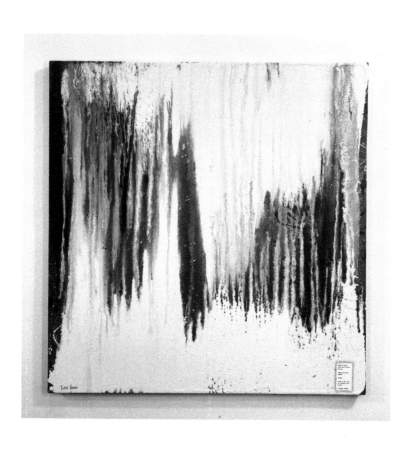

Lace up your
Chuck Taylors
and let's find
an adventure.

A New Morning

I've been down sometimes and people have
said, "Oh man, you look rough."
Or, "See, you should've just given up."

I've heard it before; I will again.
But it doesn't bother me now. Because I
know that's the lowest moment I'll
have. That moment when everyone sees me
bloodied and weak. I understand what I've
been through and why I'm on the ground
catching my breath.

I'm growing.

And I know I'll get up again. Stronger.

So if you're down today, just remember that
it's part of the growth cycle.
You'll be better after these low
moments. You'll be stronger too.

And that's a beautiful thing.

Cupcakes & Rainbows

Following your dreams
isn't cupcakes and
rainbows;
it's bloody knuckles
and dark circles
under your eyes.

I'm tired of
understanding;
I want to be
understood.

You Are An Inspiration

Your journey has been
tough at times. Late nights.
Early mornings. Tears that felt
as if they would last forever.
It is heavy. Almost impossible.
But you made it through.
And now you're on the other
side of it.

What's amazing about that story,
and what's beautiful about that path,
is now others have someone to
look to so they can also see how to
navigate the storms.

Your strength. Your courage.
Your belief that anything is possible,
is an inspiration.

Impossible To Break

Grow your voice so loud
that it becomes impossible
to not be heard.
Grow your dreams so big
that it becomes impossible
for you to keep them
to yourself.
Grow your love so wide
that it becomes impossible
for everyone not to feel it.

Grow yourself so strong
that it becomes impossible
for this world to
break you.

Hopeful Optimist

Everything is going
to be all right. I am
a hopeful optimist.
But that doesn't mean
some days won't be difficult
and some nights won't suck.

It's not about performance;
it's about perseverance.

A Better Place

Show kindness.
Spread love.
Approach situations
with empathy and
understanding.

I think that's how
the world changes
to be a better place.

A little
hippie,
a little
hillbilly,
and a whole
lot of heart.

Every Time

No. You don't know me.
You have an idea of who I am.
You've seen a glimmer
of my power. You've felt an
ounce of my pain. But you
have no idea how deep my
passion goes. You can't
imagine how hard I've fought
and what I've overcome to
be who I am today. But I know.
I remember every tear.
I count my scars like waves
in the oceans. I've been forged
in the fires of life and I
will not be broken.

So doubt me. Forget about me.
Put me down. And count me out.

And I'll keep proving you
wrong—every time.

My Time Is Now

I'm looking ahead.
I'm making no excuses.
I see the future I want and
I'm willing to work for it.
Whatever it takes.
Setbacks won't stop me.
Negative voices won't
break my spirit.
My mind is set.
My heart is willing.
Nothing is going to
stand in my way.

My time is now.

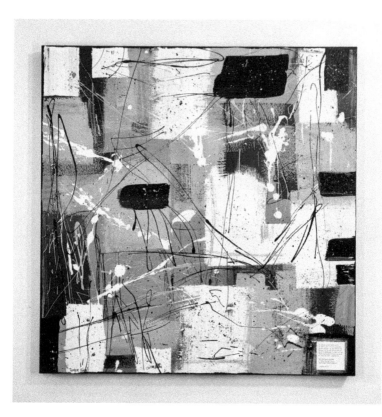

Love the one who
will dream with
you, who is up
for adventure,
and is willing
to take risks
in life.

Brighter Future

Life does not get any easier.
But we do get stronger. We
get more equipped to deal with
difficult situations.
Those hard days.
Those impossible moments.
Every time we overcome one, we
become more of the person we are
meant to be. That struggle has purpose.
That pain has a reason. Not a moment
of this journey is wasted. Not a second
of this life should be taken for granted.
Yes, there are memories that we would
rather forget and move on from. Of course
that's true. But every difficult moment is
setting us up to prove ourselves.

And to pave the way toward a
brighter future.

Rooting For You

I believe in you.
I believe in your ability
to make the world a better place.
I want you to succeed.
I want you to experience
life in a vibrant and
powerful way.

I'm rooting for you.

Memories are magic. They take us back to a time when the world made sense.

This Day

We wake. We breathe in new air.
We open our eyes and
look forward to a new day.
New opportunities.
New possibilities.
A new chance to start fresh.

This day.
These moments.
It's time to begin.
It's time to pursue
the impossible.

Something Powerful

Begin from a place of
sincerity. Of authenticity.
Introduce yourself as the
real you. Not some version
of yourself that you think
others want to know or need
to see. That only causes
more pain. Begin as you.
From the start. Establish
a genuine relationship that
is built on the foundation
of truth. And from there
grow something beautiful.

Something powerful.

Something real.

Beautiful
stories
come out of
terrible messes.

My Journey

I'm done waiting.
For the perfect moment.
Or the right time to speak.
Life is too short to give
away my time to fear or to worry.
My journey has brought me
to this place for a reason.
And I will no longer be afraid.
I'm moving forward. I'm raising my voice.
I'm telling my insecurities to step aside.
I no longer have any need for
those concerns. The future
can be anything, I'm told.

So, I plan to make it mine.

Not Afraid To Fail

Life has taught me this lesson
well and I feel like these words
are tattooed on my heart:
"I am a proud failure."
And I always will be.
I'm not afraid to fall on my face
and make a fool of myself.
Trust me, I have more times than
I care to count. But that's me.
A human who's not afraid to fail.

Love holds us
together and
nourishes our
spirits so we
can grow.

Messy

I'm a person.
I'm complicated.
I'm okay with that.
Life is messy and
strange and beautiful.

So are we.

Appreciate The Journey

I am a work in progress, yes.
But I'm also proud of the person
I am today. I've seen hard days.
I've survived long nights.
And I've learned so much
about myself through it all.

I could have quit, but I didn't.
I could have stopped, but
I kept going. I could have become
a shallow version of myself,
but I chose to grow. So, I choose
to love who I am today.

I choose to appreciate the journey.

I've learned
to love the
real me,
not just the
me that
everyone wanted
me to be.

Home

Home is a mindset.

Home is not a place. It's not where you lay your head down at night or where put your keys in a bowl. At least it's not just that.

Home is a smile. Home is a warm embrace. Home is a kiss goodnight. Home is a warm mug of coffee or a hot cup of tea in the middle of the afternoon.

Home is peace.

Home is love.

Home is being surrounded by people that understand who you really are and love you for that person. Home is that one other human who really gets you. Home is a group of friends who know you better than you know yourself.

Home is grace.

Home is forgiveness.

Home is a mindset.

Find the one
who hears
your music
the same way
you do.

Music Heals

Music heals
us in ways
that nothing
else can.

Tune Into Your Heart

They doubt you
because they have
not witnessed the
adversity you've
overcome.

Tune out the
noise of the crowd;
tune in to your
heart.

There are
some problems
in life that
only adventure
can cure.

A New Morning

A new morning.
A new day.
A new chance to prove that
life is all about standing
up again when you've been
down for a bit.

I believe in you.

Now Is Your Time

Keep dreaming. Keep planning.
Keep making people uncomfortable
with your fire. This world needs
your kind of vision. This world
needs your light. You were born
with the waves of the ocean in
your mind and the shimmer of the
universe in your heart. For too long
you were made to cover up who you really
are just to fit in to how someone else saw
the world. No longer.

Now is your time.
These are your moments.
Don't be afraid to step out,
speak up, and change the world.

Claim Your Future

Speak truth.
Create the future you want
by saying it out loud. To
yourself. So that every
ounce of you can hear it.
Yell it. Scream it so loud
that your future shakes.
Tell others your dreams.
Make a plan. Take your first
steps. And don't quit walking,
running, flying, swimming,
falling down, getting back up,
again and again until you
make it to where you want
to be. The future is yours.

It's time to claim it.

You Are Not Alone

It's important to remember that you are not alone.

You are not alone with your heavy thoughts. With the moments when you feel like it's all too much. You are not alone with your pain or your heartache. You are not alone with your healing. We are all connected in ways that we will never fully understand. But I do believe that when one of us hurts we all hurt. And when one of us feels joy we all feel joy.

We are humans. Beautiful and flawed. Complicated and wonderful. Just as we are. It's impossible to make all the right choices. It's impossible to be perfect. Because that is not how we are built. We are imperfect creatures thrown into a world that is full of struggle and questions. And we do our best to find ourselves along the way.

So the next time you have a dark thought, or a tough moment that you feel like singles you out as someone who isn't strong enough to keep going, remember that you are not alone. You are not a failure. You are a normal human being. With thoughts and struggles we all share.

Life is a messy beautiful job. But it's all worth it. And I know that our best days are still waiting to be experienced.

Trust me.
Keep going.

Also By Topher Kearby

Watercolor Words

Magnificent Mess

People You May Know

Homemade Mistakes

Life Isn't Made For Perfect People: Book 1

Contact

Email: TopherKearby@gmail.com
Facebook: @TopherKearby
Instagram: @TopherKearby
Twitter: @TopherKearby

Shop

To order artwork, a custom canvas, or
signed books, please visit Topher's
website(s) at:

www.TopherKearby.com
or
www.etsy.com/shop/TopherKearby

Thank you so much for reading this collection. If you enjoyed it, please consider leaving a review.